GW00493884

THE CREATIVE COOK

Easy

ORIENTAL

RICHARD CAWLEY

FOREWORD BY KEN HOM

PHOTOGRAPHY BY MICHELLE GARRETT

CONRAN OCTOPUS

Please note the following:
Quantities given in all the recipes serve 4 people unless otherwise stated.
Spoon measurements are level unless otherwise stated.
Metric and imperial measures are both given, use one or the other as the two are not interchangeable.
Flour used is plain white flour, unless otherwise specified.
Preparation of ingredients, such as the cleaning, trimming and peeling of vegetables and fruit, is presumed and the text only refers to any aspect of this if unusual, such as onions used unpeeled etc.
Citrus fruit is generally coated in a layer of preservative wax. For this reason, whenever a recipe uses the rind of oranges, lemons or limes the text specifies unwaxed fruit. If organic uncoated fruit is not available, scrub the fruit vigorously in hot soapy water, rinse well and pat dry.
Eggs used are size 3 (65 g/2¼ oz) unless otherwise specified. The Government recommends that eggs not be consumed raw, and people most at risk, such as children, old people, invalids and pregnant women, should not eat them lightly cooked. This book includes recipes with raw and lightly cooked eggs, which should not be eaten by the above categories. These recipes are marked by a * in the text. Once prepared, these dishes should be kept refrigerated and used promptly.

Editorial Direction: Lewis Esson Publishing
Art Director: Mary Evans
Design: Sue Storey
Illustrations: Alison Barratt
Food for Photography: Richard Cawley
Styling: Róisín Nield
Editorial Assistant: Penny David
Production Manager: Sonya Sibbons

First published in 1992 by
Conran Octopus Limited,
37 Shelton Street,
London WC2H 9HN

This new edition published in 1993 by
Conran Octopus Limited.

Text copyright © Richard Cawley
Foreword copyright © Ken Hom 1992
Photography copyright © Michelle Garrett 1992
Design and layout copyright © Conran Octopus 1992

All rights reserved. No part of this book may be reproduced, stored in a retrieval system or transmitted in any form or by any means, electronic, electrostatic, magnetic tape, mechanical, photocopying, recording or otherwise, without the prior permission in writing of the publisher.

The right of Richard Cawley to be identified as Author of this Work has been asserted by him in accordance with the Copyright, Designs and Patents Act 1988.

British Library Cataloguing in Publication Data
A catalogue record for this book is available from the British Library

ISBN 1-85029-437-2

Typeset by Hunters Armley Ltd
Printed and bound in Hong Kong.

CONTENTS

FOREWORD

This collection of recipes is a welcome addition to that genre of modern cookery that emphasizes simplicity and ease of preparation, without, however, any sacrifice of quality or delectability. There is no implication of the blandness and uniformity of 'fast food' here. All of Richard's recipes are well thought out, preserving the tastes and textures of the original cuisines. He has omitted or refashioned the more elaborate and time-consuming recipes in order to expedite the preparation of dishes and menus that capture the representative qualities of each cooking style. The essence remains intact; only the time element has changed.

Cooking quickly and easily, without compromising quality, comes naturally to those who spend a good deal of time in the kitchen. Of course, elaborate, multi-course dinners take much time and effort. But not every meal is a major social or family event, no cook *always* has enough time, and, sometimes (perhaps more often than not) a quick, easy meal is just the right thing – so long as it is also delicious. This book captures that spirit.

It is obvious that *Easy Oriental* is the fruit of many years of rich experience and successful experimentation in the kitchen. The recipes manifest Richard's personal style and good taste. I love his approach to the venerable traditions of Asian cookery. That is to say, he understands and respects both the process and the final results. As Richard's long career of teaching and writing about foods exemplifies,

there is nothing mystical about preparing the good foods of many cuisines. The art of masterful cooking requires practical understanding of both techniques and ingredients. Richard's ability to convey this understanding is one of his strong virtues.

As I peruse the recipes, many of which are familiar to me – albeit in Richard's own form – I see that he has succeeded in simplifying both the preparation and the ingredients without losing anything essential. His emphasis on freshness of ingredients and his selection of dishes that require only a few basic sauces and the most readily available seasonings together ensure that the results will be delicious and true to the original.

Let me commend, too, Richard's reliance in all of these recipes on traditional Oriental spices, seasonings and sauces. These are essential if you are to experence authentic Asian cuisine. All of the ingredients used in this book are fortunately easily available today. So take your time shopping for these exotic items, savour the adventure. Once you have stocked your pantry with the basics, you are half-way there. You need only to accumulate some experience and develop your own confidence. Using Richard's recipes as your point of departure, you will be on your way to the enjoyment of authentic healthy tasty Oriental food. I wish you good health and delicious meals!

KEN HOM

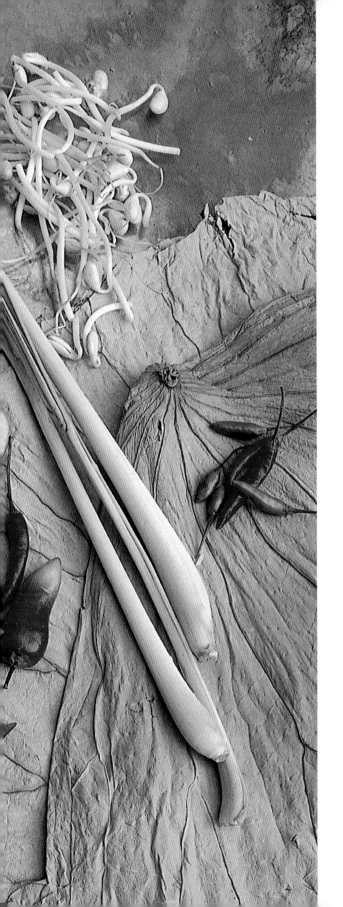

INTRODUCTION

Some years ago I spent three months travelling in China from the great cities of Shanghai and Beijing, down the Yangtse River to the end of the Great Wall on the edge of the Gobi Desert.

There were four of us, and twice a day we would order a meal consisting of five or six different dishes – over eight hundred dishes in all – and yet hardly ever did we eat the same dish twice. Chinese cooking is probably the oldest real cuisine in the world and perhaps this is the reason for its extraordinary variety.

The Chinese have always been great merchants and colonizers and their influence has spread all over South-east Asia – in the culture and food of Thailand, Malaysia and Singapore, in Korea and Japan, and south-east to the 14,000 or so islands of the Indonesian archipelago.

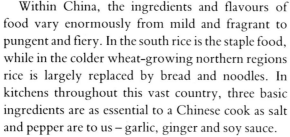

Within China, the ingredients and flavours of food vary enormously from mild and fragrant to pungent and fiery. In the south rice is the staple food, while in the colder wheat-growing northern regions rice is largely replaced by bread and noodles. In kitchens throughout this vast country, three basic ingredients are as essential to a Chinese cook as salt and pepper are to us – garlic, ginger and soy sauce.

Chinese – and indeed most Oriental food – generally takes much longer to prepare than it does to cook. In densely populated areas, the most effective way to get the best value out of small quantities of expensive fuel is to cut ingredients into small uniform bite-sized pieces, so that they need only very brief cooking. The curved-bottomed wok was developed to use the minimum amount of fat or oil and cook in the fastest possible time over the first fierce heat from a small quantity of blazing charcoal. As the coals cooled to a gentler glow, they would be economically used to cook steamed and braised dishes. Deep-frying and barbecuing complete the repertoire of classic Oriental cooking methods. Roasting and baking, which require an oven and large quantities of fuel, are hardly used at all.

The other main characteristic which distinguishes Chinese cooking is that of achieving harmony through contrast. This applies not just to the taste of food, but to its texture, shape and colour. Chinese food must please the eye as well as the palate. Japan and Thailand refined the presentation of food even further, almost to the point of being an art form.

Even though Chinese preparation techniques and cooking methods have been absorbed by the cuisines of so many other countries, each one has added its own character and personality, influenced by climate, population and local ingredients.

Religion has also played a part in shaping some Oriental cuisines. For example, most Indonesians are Muslim and shun pork, which is so greatly loved by the Chinese. Luckily, Indonesians can take advantage of the wide variety of fish from the surrounding seas. This is sometimes cooked very simply, but is often flavoured with various spices – the Indonesian archipelago was once known as the Spice Islands.

In China most food is cooked, though often very briefly. Hardly anything is eaten uncooked. However, the Japanese are passionate about raw food, especially fish and – unlike the Chinese – they also eat salads. As do the Thais, who make theirs from delicious combinations of meat and fish with fruit, vegetables and herbs. Fragrant herbs and spices, fiery chillies, pungent fish sauces and creamy coconut all help to make Thai dishes very distinctive.

Each Oriental cuisine holds its own variety of particular delights, with the added attraction for modern Western cooks that an Oriental-style diet is light and healthy, being based on rice or noodles with little fat and sugar and lots of nutritious fresh vegetables and fruit. The small quantities of meat, fish and poultry which feature on Oriental menus also mean that it is a relatively inexpensive way to eat.

ABOUT THE RECIPES

The recipes in this book are from all over the South-east Asian area, with the idea of trying to offer as much variety as possible. Many of the recipes are classics, some are adapted slightly to make them as easy as possible to cook, or to avoid difficulty in obtaining unusual ingredients. A few are my own East-meets-West favourites.

Unlike the Western habit of eating a meal of separate courses where one course follows another, most Oriental meals consist of a large communal serving of rice or noodles with a series of 'made' dishes brought to the table all at the same time. If soup is included, it may also be served at the same time to be enjoyed throughout the meal, rather than as a first course.

The idea of this book is that you should mix and match whichever dishes you wish, in whichever order you like – or all at once in the style of a Chinese banquet. Don't feel you should choose all the dishes from one area – it is interesting and fun to mix dishes from different countries in one meal.

Do try and select recipes which will give you 'harmony through contrast', but be careful not to choose too many dishes which require last-minute cooking. Many dishes – especially soups, salads and dishes cooked in sauces – may be prepared a little in advance to help spread the work-load. A menu consisting solely of deep-fried and stir-fried dishes will not leave the cook much time to sit down and enjoy the food or company.

If you are new to this kind of cooking, perhaps you might like to try just one or two Oriental dishes to begin with, incorporating just one dish at a time into a Western-style meal. Try serving a Chinese soup or a Thai salad as a starter before a traditional roast dinner, for instance. If you fancy mashed potatoes with spare ribs instead of rice, go ahead – remember food is to be enjoyed.

If you are undecided what to drink with an Oriental meal, the safest bet is cold beer, as it will not be overpowered by spicy flavours in the way that a delicate wine might be. Dry sherry – which is very like Chinese wine, is excellent served with snacks and aperitifs at the beginning of a meal. Chinese tea and mineral waters make good non-alcoholic alternatives.

INGREDIENTS AND EQUIPMENT

Most of the ingredients used in these recipes can be found in large supermarkets and most large towns now have an Oriental supermarket. If you have trouble finding any of the more unusual items, Exotic Speciality Food Limited (see page 64) have an extensive mail order catalogue and will be able to supply anything you might need. You will find notes on more unusual ingredients alongside the appropriate recipes, plus suggested substitutes.

Many of the recipes include fresh chilli peppers. There are many different sizes, shapes and colours of chillies available and all vary in 'heat'. As a general rule, the smaller they are the more fiery their flavour. The only certain way to find out is to taste a tiny piece and judge for yourself how much to put in. The quantities given in the recipes are only suggestions and whether you choose to use more or less is a matter of taste. The seeds are the hottest part of the pepper, so it is advisable to remove these during preparation. It is also a good idea to wear rubber gloves when preparing chillies, as the slightest touch of a 'chilli finger' on eyes, or other sensitive parts of the body, can cause extreme discomfort. Otherwise, be sure to wash your hands carefully after handling the chillies.

A wok is almost essential for cooking most Oriental dishes. Comparatively cheap woks are, however, readily available in most cookware shops and prove invaluable in the kitchen for all kinds of cooking apart from just Eastern recipes. Stir-frying with a wok is a very healthy way to cook as it uses very little oil. The important thing to remember when using a wok is to heat it well before putting in the oil. Wait until you can feel the heat radiating from the base of the interior when you place your hand about 7.5 cm/3 in above it. When deep-frying in a wok, pour in enough oil to give a depth of about 5 cm/2 in and heat it over a moderate heat until you can just see a faint haze of smoke rising from it before putting in the food to be fried. Cook in fairly small batches so that the wok is not overcrowded and the food doesn't cool the oil too much when it is added.

So stock your pantry with a few Oriental herbs, spices and condiments; pile your shopping basket with delicious fresh ingredients; get out your wok and fill your kitchen with the delicious aromas and flavours of the Orient.

Thick sweet spicy PLUM SAUCE *is traditionally served by the Chinese as a dip with dumplings or seafood and with poultry dishes, especially duck.* ORIENTAL 'PRESERVED BOTTLED PLUMS', *pickled in a spiced vinegar, are available from Oriental supermarkets. A blender or food processor easily gets the peppers chopped to the correct degree of fineness.*

SAMBALS *are Indonesian relishes, usually spiced with chilli peppers.*

PLUM SAUCE

55g/2 oz Oriental 'Preserved Bottled Plums'
450 g/1 lb granulated sugar
2–3 large red chilli peppers, deseeded and very finely chopped
1 red sweet pepper, deseeded and very finely chopped
4 tbsp malt or white wine vinegar

Rub the plums through the fingers to break up the flesh, but do not discard the stones.

Put the sugar and 300 ml/10 fl oz of water in a medium saucepan and bring to the boil over a moderate heat. When the syrup is boiling well add the chopped chilli peppers, the sweet pepper and the plums with their stones. Bring back to the boil and allow to boil for 2-3 minutes, then add the vinegar. The resulting sauce will be sweet-and-sour.

Allow to cool, remove the stones and discard. Pour into warmed sterile bottles or jars and seal or tightly stopper. This sauce will stay fresh for several weeks in the refrigerator.

CUCUMBER AND CARROT RELISH

2 tbsp sugar
juice of ½ lime
¼ cucumber, finely chopped
2 shallots, thinly sliced
1 small carrot, grated
1 large red or green chilli pepper or more to taste, deseeded and finely chopped

In a small bowl, dissolve the sugar in 2 tablespoons of hot water. Mix in all the other ingredients.

Leave for at least an hour to allow the flavours to develop fully, but use within 24 hours. Keep refrigerated.

PEANUT AND PEPPER RELISH

115 g/4 oz salted peanuts, chopped
½ red or yellow sweet pepper, deseeded and finely chopped
½ tsp curry powder
1 small garlic clove, crushed
3 tbsp Greek yogurt
2 tbsp chopped flat-leaf parsley

Mix all the ingredients and chill for at least 1 hour, or up to 24, to allow the flavours to develop fully.

MANGO SAMBAL

½ large ripe mango, peeled and coarsely chopped
2 spring onions, thinly sliced
⅛ cucumber, coarsely chopped
1 chilli pepper, deseeded and finely chopped
juice of 1 lime or lemon
1 heaped tbsp chopped coriander

Combine all the ingredients except the coriander and chill for at least 1 hour, or up to 24, to allow the flavours to develop fully.

Just before serving, mix in the coriander.

COCONUT SAMBAL

85 g/3 oz freshly grated coconut
55 g/2 oz mild onions, thinly sliced
1 chilli pepper, deseeded and finely chopped
juice of 1 lime or lemon
¼ tsp salt

Mix all the ingredients together well and chill for at least 1 hour, or up to 24, to allow the flavours to develop fully.

SPICED BANANA SALAD

30 g/1 oz unsalted butter
1 tsp black cumin seed
¼ tsp chilli powder
2 firm bananas, peeled and cut into 1 cm/½ in slices
2 small heads of chicory, separated into leaves
1 small mild onion, very thinly sliced and separated into rings
4 tbsp natural yogurt
salt
cayenne pepper

Melt the butter in a frying pan over a moderate heat and fry the cumin and chilli powder for 2 minutes.

Add the banana slices and fry for 2-3 minutes, turning once. The banana should be soft and hot, but still hold its shape.

Arrange the chicory leaves on 4 small plates or bowls, radiating out from the centre. Add the onion rings and the warm banana and sprinkle with salt to taste.

Top with the yogurt, sprinkle with cayenne and serve immediately.

NOTE: alternatively present the entire dish on one large serving platter. Serve as a side-dish with any curry.

Clockwise from the top: Coconut Sambal, Mango Sambal, Plum Sauce, Peanut and Pepper Relish, Cucumber and Carrot Relish

SNACKS, STARTERS AND SOUPS

Outdoor stalls all over the countries of the Far East sell all kinds of 'fast food', which may be eaten sitting at nearby wooden benches, or while walking along the street. A selection of these Oriental 'snacks' can make an original first course for any meal, either Oriental- or Western-style. They also make perfect finger-food for drinks parties or buffets. Soups are just as popular in the Far East as they are here. They are not usually served at the beginning of a meal, however, but are generally brought to the table with all the other dishes and are dipped into throughout the meal. Nevertheless, most of their soups do adapt perfectly to Western eating habits and make ideal first courses or light lunch or supper dishes.

Clockwise from the left: Pot Sticker Dumplings (page 14), Little Barbecue Pork Patties (page 21) and Sesame Prawn Toasts (page 14)

POT STICKER
DUMPLINGS *are a*
popular Chinese
snack often included
in the 'dim sum'
menus traditional to
family Sunday
lunches, which
feature dumplings of
all types – steamed,
grilled and fried.

SESAME PRAWN TOASTS

MAKES 24

225 g/8 oz raw prawns in their shells, heads removed
30 g/1 oz canned Chinese water chestnuts, drained
30 g/1 oz streaky bacon, chopped
½ tsp salt
1 tsp cornflour
white of 1 small egg
6 slices of white bread, crusts removed
4 tbsp sesame seeds
vegetable oil, for frying

Remove the shells from the prawns. Using a sharp knife, make an incision along the length of the back of each prawn (the outside curve). Remove and discard any dark thread, or gut.

Place the prawn meat, water chestnuts, bacon, salt, cornflour and egg white in the bowl of a blender or food processor and reduce to a smooth purée.

Alternatively, reduce the ingredients to a purée in a large mortar with a pestle, or simply chop them as fine as possible with a sharp knife.

Spread the purée evenly over the slices of bread.

Spread an even layer of sesame seeds on a large plate and then press the spread sides of the bread on them to coat them evenly with seeds.

Fill a frying pan or wok with oil to a depth of about 2.5 cm/1 in. Heat until nice and hot, then fry the toasts, coated side down, for about 1 minute or so, until the seeds are crisp and golden. Turn and fry on the other side until the bread is crisp and golden. Drain on paper towels.

Cut each slice into 4 even strips and serve as soon as possible.

POT STICKER DUMPLINGS

MAKES 16

170 g/6 oz flour
2 tbsp vegetable oil
150 ml/¼ pt chicken or vegetable stock
sweet chilli sauce or other dipping sauce, to serve
FOR THE FILLING
85 g/3 oz white crab meat
30 g/1 oz white cabbage, finely chopped
1 small spring onion, finely chopped
2.5 cm/1 in cube of peeled fresh root ginger, finely chopped
1 tbsp dry sherry
1 tbsp soy sauce
¼ tsp salt
1 tsp sesame oil
½ tsp sugar

In a bowl, mix the flour with 125 ml/4 fl oz of very hot water to make a dough. Knead for 10 minutes, adding a little more water if the dough seems too dry or a little more flour if it seems too sticky. Cover with a damp cloth and leave to rest for 30 minutes.

Meanwhile, make the filling: mix all the ingredients together in a bowl.

Knead the rested dough again for 5 minutes and divide it into 16 equal balls. On a floured surface, roll the balls out to make circles of dough with a diameter of about 7.5 cm/3 in. Keep the balls and circles of dough covered with a damp cloth while working to prevent them drying out.

Place a small teaspoon of stuffing in the centre of each circle of dough. Moisten the edges with water. Fold each circle over in half to make a semi-circle and pinch the edges to seal. Using the thumb and forefinger, 'frill' the edges to make each dumpling into a small Cornish pasty shape, with a frilly seam on top and a flat bottom.

Heat the oil in a frying or sauté pan which is large enough to take the dumplings snugly in one layer and preferably has a tight-fitting lid. Fry the dumplings over a very low heat or until their flat bottoms are crisp and golden.

Pour over the stock, cover and simmer over a very low heat for 12-15 minutes, or until all the liquid has been absorbed. Remove the lid and cook for a further 2 minutes.

Serve hot, accompanied by sweet chilli sauce or another dipping sauce.

THAI FISH CAKES

MAKES 8

225 g/8 oz skinless white fish fillets, coarsely chopped
1½ tsp Thai red curry paste
1 tbsp cornflour
1 tbsp fish sauce
1 small egg, beaten
1 large red or green chilli pepper, deseeded and chopped
2 shallots, finely chopped
85 g/3 oz thin French beans, finely chopped
2 tbsp vegetable oil
Cucumber and Carrot Relish (see page 10) or a dipping sauce, to serve

In a blender or food processor, blend the fish until just smooth. Add the curry paste, cornflour, fish sauce and egg and process briefly until mixed. Be careful not to over-process, or the fish will lose all texture! Transfer to a small bowl and mix in the chilli pepper, shallots and beans.

Divide the mixture into 8 portions and shape them into round cakes about 6 mm/¼ in thick.

Heat the oil in a frying pan over a moderate heat and fry the cakes for 3-4 minutes on each side, until uniformly golden.

Serve immediately with Cucumber and Carrot Relish or a dipping sauce.

DEEP-FRIED 'SEAWEED'

225 g/8 oz cabbage greens, very finely shredded
vegetable oil, for deep-frying
sugar, for sprinkling

Heat the oil in a wok until just beginning to smoke, then deep-fry the shredded cabbage in small batches for a few seconds only, until it turns dark and crispy.

Remove each batch with a slotted spoon, drain on paper towels and keep warm while the remaining batches are being cooked.

Serve sprinkled with a little sugar as soon as all the greens are cooked.

THAI RED CURRY PASTE is flavoured with lime zest, lemon grass, galangal and trassi – the South-east Asian condiment made from fermented shrimp – and is available from Oriental suppliers.

As here, the DEEP-FRIED 'SEAWEED' served in many Chinese restaurants is not seaweed at all but shredded greens. Use a food processor to shred them very finely.

Popular in Singapore, Malaysia and Indonesia, SATAY dishes consist of tiny 'kebabs' and may contain meat, poultry or fish.

Japanese TERIYAKI SAUCE, made from soy beans and wine and used as a marinade and basting sauce, is available bottled from Oriental shops, as are small wooden skewers.

CHICKEN SATAY

MAKES 8 SMALL SKEWERS

225 g/8 oz skinless chicken breast, cut into 2 cm/¾ in cubes
FOR THE MARINADE
1 tbsp brown sugar
2 tbsp soy sauce
juice of ½ lemon
1 tbsp vegetable oil
FOR THE DIPPING SAUCE
1 tbsp vegetable oil
1 small onion, finely chopped
1 garlic clove, crushed
1 tbsp crunchy peanut butter
1 tbsp sweet chilli sauce
1 tsp soy sauce
3 tbsp boiling water

First make the marinade: in a small bowl, dissolve the sugar in 1 tablespoon of hot water and then add the remaining ingredients and mix well. Add the chicken pieces and stir until well coated, then leave for at least 1 hour, or up to 24 hours in the refrigerator.

Meanwhile make the dipping sauce: in a small pan, heat the oil over a moderate heat and cook the onion until softened. Then add the remaining ingredients and simmer for 3 minutes. Transfer to a serving bowl and allow to cool.

Soak 8 small wooden skewers in water for 30 minutes or more, to prevent them scorching too much during cooking. Preheat a hot grill or barbecue.

Thread the marinated meat on the prepared skewers and cook them under the grill or on the barbecue for 4-5 minutes, turning once.

Serve accompanied by the dipping sauce.

Note: for an unusual and attractive presentation use bay twigs instead of skewers.

TERIYAKI CHICKEN

MAKES 12 SKEWERS

2 tbsp vegetable oil
5 tbsp Teriyaki sauce
1 tbsp dry sherry
1 tbsp brown sugar
1 garlic clove, crushed
2.5 cm/1 in cube of peeled fresh root ginger, crushed in a garlic press or very finely chopped
½ small red sweet pepper, deseeded and cut into 1 cm/½ in squares
225 g/8 oz skinned chicken breast, cut into 1 cm/½ in cubes
strips of spring onion and cucumber, to serve

Soak 12 small wooden skewers in water for 30 minutes or more, to prevent them from scorching too much under the hot grill.

Place all the ingredients except the chicken, spring onion and cucumber in a bowl and mix them well to combine.

Drop the pieces of chicken into the marinade and toss them well in the mixture to ensure that they are coated on all sides. Cover and leave for at least 30 minutes, or up to 3 hours, shaking the bowl occasionally.

Preheat a hot grill or barbecue.

Thread the pieces of chicken and pepper on the skewers and grill or barbecue for about 5 minutes, or until cooked through, turning 2 or 3 times and brushing each time with marinade.

Serve immediately, accompanied by the spring onion and cucumber.

Clockwise from the bottom left: Teriyaki Chicken, Chicken Satay and Water Chestnuts in Crispy Bacon (page 20)

THAI STUFFED CHICKEN WINGS

MAKES 12

12 chicken wings (see below)
115 g/4 oz minced pork
55 g/2 oz canned bamboo shoots, drained
55 g/2 oz canned Chinese water chestnuts, drained
30 g/1 oz button mushrooms
2 garlic cloves, crushed
2 tsp dark soy sauce
1 tsp sugar
1 egg, lightly beaten
4 tbsp flour
salt and freshly ground black pepper
vegetable oil, for deep-frying and greasing
Plum Sauce (see page 10), to serve

Try to buy wings with 2 joints. Cut off the bits furthest from the tip, skin them and take the flesh from the bones. Mince this flesh and add it to the pork in a large bowl. If wings with only the wing tip and 1 joint are all that is available, buy another 115 g/4 oz minced chicken and add this to the pork.

Chop the bamboo shoots, water chestnuts and mushrooms very finely in a food processor and add to the meat mixture, together with the garlic, soy sauce, sugar and a good seasoning of salt and pepper. Mix very well together and then add the egg to bind and mix well again

Using a small sharp pointed knife, bone the wings, working from the cut end. There are two bones, one bigger than the other, which will be joined together at that cut end. Separate them first with the point of the knife. The bigger bone will also be firmly attached to the flesh on the side opposite to the small bone – carefully detach this with the knife.

Now using the edge of the knife, scrape the flesh

Top: Sesame Beef Balls; bottom: Thai Stuffed Chicken Wings

downward from the bones, being careful not to cut the skin. Work down to the joint, then twist and snap each bone off in turn. Discard these bones or reserve them for stock. This will leave wing tips with a hollow pocket of skin and meat attached.

Using a teaspoon and the fingers, fill the cavities with the minced meat mixture. They should be filled until they are almost overflowing.

Place the stuffed wings in the lightly oiled upper part of a steamer and steam over boiling water for 20 minutes, or until firm. Allow to cool

Season the flour with salt and pepper. Coat the cooled wings in it and deep-fry them in batches in hot oil in a wok until the skin is golden brown and nicely crisp. Drain on paper towels and keep warm while the rest are being cooked.

Serve immediately with Plum Sauce.

SESAME BEEF BALLS

350 g/12 oz very lean minced beef
45 g/1½ oz rindless streaky bacon, chopped
1 tbsp chopped celery
1 tbsp chopped carrot
1 tbsp finely chopped mushroom
2 spring onions, chopped
1 tbsp cornflour
1 tbsp soy sauce
1 tbsp sherry
½ tsp salt
1 egg, beaten
2 tbsp bottled hoi-sin sauce
2 tsp sugar
1 tbsp sesame seeds
freshly ground black pepper
flour, for dusting
vegetable oil, for deep-frying
hoi-sin sauce, Plum Sauce (see page 10) or other dipping
sauce, to serve

Put the minced beef, bacon, chopped vegetables, mushrooms, spring onions, cornflour, two-thirds of the soy sauce, the sherry, salt and some pepper in a blender or food processor and process until well mixed. Be careful not to over-process.

Using floured hands, form the paste into walnut-sized balls. Coat these thoroughly and evenly in the beaten egg.

Deep-fry the coated balls in hot oil in a wok until well browned all over. Drain the cooked balls on paper towels.

Remove all but 2 tablespoons of the oil from the pan and add the remaining soy sauce, the hoi-sin sauce, sugar and sesame seeds.

Heat the pan over a moderate heat, add the beef balls and cook for a few minutes, shaking the pan occasionally until the balls are coated with the sauces and sesame seeds and turn a deep mahogany brown all over.

Serve immediately with more hoi-sin sauce, Plum Sauce or other dipping sauce.

Fresh CHINESE WATER CHESTNUTS are occasionally available from Chinese markets.

HOI-SIN SAUCE, one of the most popular dipping sauces in China, is available in bottles from most better supermarkets.

SPRING ROLL *wrappers are available fresh or frozen from Oriental suppliers, as are* CHINESE DRIED MUSHROOMS.

ORIENTAL SESAME OIL *differs from the sesame oil sold in health food shops as it is made from toasted sesame seeds to give much greater flavour.*

WATER CHESTNUTS IN CRISPY BACON

200 g/7 oz smoked streaky bacon, rinds removed
225 g/8 oz canned Chinese water chestnuts, drained

Soak some wooden toothpicks in water for 30 minutes or more to prevent them from burning during cooking. Preheat a hot grill.

Using the back of a knife, scrape each slice of bacon to stretch it a little and then cut it across into 2 even lengths.

Wrap each water chestnut in a length of bacon and secure with one of the toothpicks.

Grill the parcels for 5-7 minutes, turning once, until the bacon is crispy.

Serve immediately.

SPRING ROLLS

MAKES 12

12 spring roll wrappers
vegetable oil, for deep-frying
FOR THE FILLING
5 dried Chinese mushrooms
1 tbsp vegetable oil
½ tsp Oriental sesame oil
225 g/8 oz minced pork
2 spring onions, finely chopped
2 garlic cloves, crushed
1 small carrot, grated
6 canned Chinese water chestnuts, drained and chopped
75 g/2½ oz peeled cooked prawns, chopped
1 tbsp soy sauce
1 egg, beaten

Soak the dried mushrooms in warm water for 30 minutes. Drain, remove and discard the stalks and slice the caps thinly.

Make the filling: heat the oils in a wok or frying pan over a moderate heat and stir-fry the pork for 5 minutes. Add the onions, garlic, carrot, mushrooms and water chestnuts and continue to stir-fry for 2 minutes. Allow the mixture to cool.

Add the prawns, soy sauce and most of the egg to the mixture, saving a little egg to seal the wrappers.

Divide the mixture into 12 portions and place one on the edge of each pastry wrapper. Fold in the sides of each and roll it up, brushing the join with a little of the reserved egg to seal.

Deep-fry the rolls in batches in hot oil in a wok for about 4-5 minutes each, or until golden and crispy. Be careful not to have the fat too hot or the skins will burn before the filling is cooked through. Drain on paper towels and keep warm while the rest are being cooked. Serve as soon as all are cooked.

NOTE: serve with a dipping sauce made from equal parts soy sauce and wine vinegar.

LITTLE BARBECUE PORK PATTIES

MAKES 16

55 g/2 oz Chinese barbecue pork (see below),
very finely chopped
1 tbsp vegetable oil
55 g/2 oz spring onions, finely chopped
2 tsp oyster sauce
1 tsp dark soy sauce
1 tsp sugar
½ tsp salt
25 g/¾ oz cornflour
4 tbsp chicken stock
1 egg yolk
1 tbsp milk
2 tbsp sesame seeds
sweet chilli sauce or a bottled dipping sauce, to serve
FOR THE PASTRY
115 g/4 oz plain flour
pinch of salt
55 g/2 oz butter, cut into small pieces

Barbecue pork is available from Chinese restaurants and take-aways.

Preheat the oven to 220C/425F/gas7.

First make the pastry: in a bowl mix the flour and salt and then rub in the butter until the mixture resembles fine breadcrumbs. Add just enough cold water to form a dough. Knead well and chill for 30 minutes.

Meanwhile make the filling: heat the oil in a wok over a low heat and soften the spring onions in it briefly. Mix them with the pork, sauces, sugar and salt in a small pan.

Mix the cornflour to a paste with a few drops of the stock, then add the remaining stock. Mix this into the contents of the pan. Bring to the boil and simmer over a low heat, stirring constantly until thickened. Allow the mixture to cool completely.

Roll out the pastry very thinly and cut out sixteen 7.5 cm/3 in rounds, re-rolling the trimmings as necessary.

Put a teaspoon of filling in the centre of each circle, slightly dampen the edges of the pastry with a very little water and fold in half to form little half-moon-shaped patties. Pinch the edges together well to seal them and arrange the patties on a baking sheet.

Mix the egg yolk and milk and brush the patties with a little of this mixture. Sprinkle them with sesame seeds and bake for 15 minutes, or until crisp and golden brown.

Serve immediately, accompanied by sweet chilli sauce or a bottled dipping sauce.

OYSTER SAUCE, although made from oysters, does not taste fishy but is used to give depth of flavour to a wide variety of dishes and is available in bottles from Oriental shops and large supermarkets. Several varieties of chilli sauce are available from Oriental suppliers. The SWEET CHILLI SAUCE called for in many recipes contains tomatoes and sugar and is mild in flavour.

MICHAEL'S THAI BEEF SOUP

The recipe for this delicious main-course soup was given to me by the chef at my local Thai restaurant. FRESH CORIANDER *leaves are usually sold complete with their stems and roots which make useful flavourings.* STAR ANISE *is a pungent star-shaped spice with a strong aniseed flavour.*

8 garlic cloves
675 g/1½ lb piece of beef skirt or other good braising beef
4 tbsp chopped coriander root and stem
6 heads of star anise
2 carrots, chopped
2 celery stalks, chopped
1 onion, chopped
2 tbsp soy sauce
1 tbsp Maggi sauce or 1 beef stock cube
1 tbsp brown sugar
2 tsp salt
350 g/12 oz Chinese noodles
225 g/8 oz beansprouts
about 4 tbsp fish sauce
¼ tsp chilli powder
2 spring onions, chopped
vegetable oil, for deep-frying
coriander leaves, to garnish

Coarsely chop 4 garlic cloves and slice the rest.

Put the beef in a large saucepan with the coarsely chopped garlic, the coriander root, star anise, carrots, celery, onion, soy sauce, Maggi sauce or stock cube, sugar, salt and 1.75 litre/3 pt of water. Bring to the boil and simmer for 40 minutes.

Remove the meat from the stock and allow it to cool slightly. When cool enough to handle, cut it into thin bite-sized pieces and keep these warm.

Cook the noodles according to the instructions. Blanch the beansprouts in boiling salted water for 1 minute only. Deep-fry the garlic slices in hot oil in a wok or small pan until golden and drain.

Strain the soup into a clean pan, warm through and add the fish sauce and chilli powder to taste.

Put the beansprouts in 4 warmed soup bowls. Arrange the noodles, meat and spring onions on top.

Ladle the soup into the bowls and garnish with the garlic and coriander. Serve with spoons and forks.

The flavour of THAI PRAWN SOUP *relies on fragrant* LEMON GRASS *and* KAFFIR LIME LEAVES *which add a strong citrus note without acidity. These are available, fresh or dried, from Oriental shops or by mail order (see page 64). Lemon or lime rind may be used instead, but will not give the same distinctive taste.* GALANGAL, *a spice related to ginger, is available from Oriental suppliers and by mail order as above. Fresh ginger may be substituted.*

QUICK CHICKEN AND COCONUT SOUP

450 ml/¾ pt chicken stock
grated zest and juice of ½ unwaxed lime,
plus juice of 1 more lime
3 tbsp fish sauce
1 tsp ground ginger
½ tsp chilli powder
300 ml/½ pt thick coconut milk
170 g/6 oz skinned boneless chicken breasts, cut across into thin slices
chopped fresh coriander, to garnish
sliced deseeded chilli peppers, to garnish (optional)

Put the stock in a saucepan with the lime zest and juice, the fish sauce, ginger and chilli powder and simmer for 5 minutes.

Add the coconut milk and chicken slices and simmer for 2 or 3 more minutes, until the chicken is just cooked through.

Pour into 4 warmed bowls and garnish with coriander and chilli slices, if using.

THAI PRAWN SOUP

350 g/12 oz raw prawns in their shells, heads removed
3 chilli peppers
1 tbsp vegetable oil
2 stalks of lemon grass, thinly sliced
3 Kaffir lime leaves
3 slices of galangal, each about 1 cm/½ in thick
2 garlic cloves, chopped
2 tbsp fish sauce, or more according to taste
juice of ½ lime
1 tbsp chopped coriander, to garnish
3 chopped spring onions, to garnish

Remove the shells from the prawns, put the meat to one side and reserve the shells. Deseed the chilli peppers. Coarsely chop 2 of them and thinly slice the third.

Heat the oil in a saucepan over a moderate heat and fry the prawn shells for 1-2 minutes, or until they turn pink.

Add 1.5 litre/2½ pt of water, the coarsely chopped chilli peppers, the lemon grass, Kaffir lime leaves, galangal, garlic and fish sauce. Bring to the boil, reduce the heat and simmer for 20 minutes. Strain into a clean pan and discard the solids.

Add the shelled prawns and cook for 3-4 minutes, or until the prawns are just cooked through. Do not overcook or the prawns will become tough and tasteless.

Add the lime juice and, if the soup seems too bland, add a little more fish sauce to taste.

Pour into 4 warmed bowls and garnish with the slices of chilli pepper, the coriander and the chopped spring onion.

SWEETCORN AND CRAB SOUP*

850 ml/1½ pt chicken stock
*1 cm/½ in cube of peeled fresh root ginger, crushed through
a garlic press or very finely chopped*
1 tsp soy sauce
1 tsp sugar
*350 g/12 oz canned or frozen sweetcorn kernels, drained
or defrosted*
1 tbsp cornflour
3 tbsp dry sherry
170 g/6 oz canned crab meat, drained
white of 1 egg, lightly beaten
*(*see page 2 for advice on eggs)*
1 tsp sesame oil
55 g/2 oz chopped cooked ham, to garnish (optional)
1 thinly sliced spring onion, to garnish

Put the chicken stock in a saucepan with the ginger, soy sauce, sugar and sweetcorn. Bring to the boil and then reduce the heat and simmer the mixture for 2–3 minutes.

In a small bowl, mix the cornflour with the sherry. Remove the pan from the heat and whisk the cornflour mixture into the soup. Simmer for 2 minutes more, until the soup thickens.

Add the crab meat and cook for another minute or so to warm it through.

Remove the soup from the heat once more. Whisk the egg white with the sesame oil and then vigorously whisk this into the soup so that it forms white strands.

Pour into 4 warmed bowls and sprinkle with chopped ham, if using, and the chopped spring onion.

HOT AND SOUR SOUP

4 Chinese dried mushrooms
1.1 litre/2 pt chicken stock
115 g/4 oz chicken breast fillet, cut into thin slivers
85 g/3 oz peeled cooked prawns
115 g/4 oz tofu, cut into 1 cm/½ in cubes
*55 g/2 oz canned bamboo shoots, drained and cut into short
pieces*
55 g/2 oz frozen peas
2 spring onions, chopped
2 tbsp soy sauce
3 tbsp white wine vinegar
2 tbsp cornflour
salt and freshly ground black pepper
1 tsp Oriental sesame oil, to serve

Soak the dried mushrooms in warm water for 30 minutes. Drain them, remove and discard the stalks and slice the caps thinly.

Bring the stock to the boil in a saucepan, add the mushrooms and chicken and simmer the mixture for 10 minutes.

Add the prawns, tofu, bamboo shoots, peas and spring onions and simmer the mixture for 2 more minutes.

In a bowl, mix together the soy sauce, vinegar, cornflour and 85 ml/3 fl oz of water. Season with salt and plenty of pepper to give the soup its characteristic 'hot' flavour.

Stir this mixture into the soup and simmer for another 2 minutes until the soup thickens.

Pour the soup into warmed bowls and add a few drops of sesame oil to each to serve.

A wide variety of bottled FISH SAUCES *is made from fermented fish by various Oriental nations. This salty condiment, used as a flavour enhancer and not just in fish dishes, is available from Oriental supermarkets.*

TOFU, *or soy bean curd, is available from better supermarkets and health-food shops as well as Oriental supermarkets.*

MAIN COURSE DISHES

*T*he Oriental style of eating is quite different from our traditional concept of 'meat and two veg' main courses. Instead, an Oriental meal will usually consist of a central dish of rice or noodles accompanied by a variety of 'made' dishes. These might be only a couple of stir-fries for a simple family meal, or there could be a succession of countless elaborate recipes for a banquet or special occasion. Whatever the type of meal, however, the balance of ingredients will invariably tip heavily towards fresh vegetables, grains and fruit, with meat, poultry and fish appearing in much smaller quantities than is generally the case in the West. For this reason alone, the Oriental diet is a very healthy one.

Many of the dishes in this chapter may be served as Western-style main courses with accompanying rice and vegetables.

Dover Sole with Mushrooms and Pork (page 28) served with plainly cooked white rice

SESAME-CRUMBED SALMON WITH GINGER CREAM *is a particularly fine East-meets-West recipe as it provides a simple and different way of cooking salmon to bring out the best of its delicate flavour.*

DRIED CHINESE BLACK MUSHROOMS *are very similar to dried French ceps and Italian porcini.*

SESAME-CRUMBED SALMON WITH GINGER CREAM

55 g/2 oz sesame seeds
1 egg, beaten
4 skinless salmon fillets, each weighing 115–140 g/4–5 oz
3 tbsp vegetable oil
flour, for coating
salt and freshly ground black pepper
FOR THE SAUCE
300 ml/½ pt single cream
4 cm/1½ in cube of peeled fresh root ginger, crushed through a garlic press
1 tbsp light soy sauce or more to taste

Toast the sesame seeds in a dry frying pan over a low to moderate heat until lightly coloured and aromatic. Put the toasted sesame seeds, beaten egg and some flour in 3 separate shallow dishes.

Season the fish fillets on both sides with salt and pepper. Dip them first in the flour, shaking off the excess, then dip them in the egg and finally in the toasted sesame seeds.

Heat the oil in a frying pan over a moderate to low heat and fry the coated fish for 2-3 minutes on each side, until crisp and golden and cooked through.

Meanwhile, make the sauce: combine the cream, ginger and soy sauce in a small saucepan and simmer them for 2-3 minutes. Add a little more soy sauce to taste, if necessary.

Serve accompanied by plainly cooked rice or noodles and fresh steamed or boiled vegetables.

DOVER SOLE WITH MUSHROOMS AND PORK

45 g/1½ oz dried Chinese black mushrooms
1 whole Dover sole, weighing about 500 g/1 lb 2 oz, skinned
1 tsp cornflour
2 tsp dry sherry
½ tsp Oriental sesame oil, plus more for greasing
¼ tsp soy sauce
1 tsp oyster sauce
45 g/1½ oz shredded lean pork
1 slice of bacon, cut across into thin strips
1 cm/½ in cube of peeled fresh root ginger, cut into fine julienne strips
1 small spring onion, thinly sliced, to garnish
chopped fresh coriander, to garnish

Soak the mushrooms in warm water for 30 minutes. Drain them thoroughly, cut off and discard the stalks and thinly slice the caps.

Arrange the fish in a steamer. (First placing 2 strips of lightly oiled foil in a cross shape in the bottom of the pan will make it easier to remove the fish when it is cooked.)

Blend the cornflour with a little sherry and then mix this thoroughly with the remaining sherry, sesame oil, soy and oyster sauces, pork, bacon and ginger.

Spoon this mixture on top of the fish and steam it over boiling water until the flesh flakes readily. This will depend on the fish, but could be anything from 10 to 15 minutes.

Transfer the fish to a warmed serving plate and garnish with the spring onion and coriander.

CHILLI PRAWNS IN PINEAPPLES

2 small ripe pineapples
1 tbsp vegetable oil
1 onion, chopped
1 garlic clove, crushed
1 large or 2 small stalks of celery, coarsely chopped
2 tbsp chopped sweet pepper (preferably red)
1 tsp chilli powder or more to taste
200 ml/7 fl oz chicken stock
2 heaped tsp arrowroot, dissolved in a little water
350 g/12 oz peeled cooked prawns
115 g/4 oz small seedless grapes (any colour or mixed)
salt and freshly ground black pepper
55 g/2 oz blanched split almonds, grilled or dry-fried until golden, to garnish
4 large or 8 medium cooked prawns in their shells, to garnish

Cut the pineapples in half lengthwise, including the crown of green leaves. Being careful not to cut through the skin, cut out all the flesh and set the shells aside in a warm place. Cut the flesh into bite-sized pieces, discarding any hard core, and set the flesh aside.

Heat the oil in a large saucepan and cook the onion until translucent. Add the garlic, celery, sweet pepper and chilli powder with salt and pepper to taste. Stir-fry the mixture for 2-3 minutes until the vegetables are softened.

Stir in the stock, bring to the boil and simmer for 15 minutes. Add the arrowroot mixture and stir well until the mixture is thickened.

Add the peeled prawns, grapes and pineapple pieces and continue to cook gently until these are just heated through. (The prawns will toughen if cooked too long.)

Pile the cooked prawn mixture into the reserved pineapple half shells and garnish with grilled or fried almonds and the cooked prawns in their shells.

For a striking buffet party dish serve the CHILLI PRAWNS IN PINEAPPLES *in one or two half shells from a large pineapple. A wide variety of seafood suits this treatment: try using scallops or crab meat.*

SPICED CRAB CLAWS

2 tbsp vegetable oil
8 large or 12 medium shelled crab claws, defrosted if frozen
1 small onion, finely chopped
2 garlic cloves, crushed
2 chilli peppers, finely chopped
4 cm/1½ in cube of peeled fresh root ginger, finely chopped
½ tsp ground coriander seeds
1 tsp sugar
1 tbsp soy sauce
2 tsp tomato paste
juice of ½ lime
salt

Shelled crab claws can be bought frozen from Oriental supermarkets.

In a frying pan or wok, heat the oil over a moderate heat and fry the crab claws for 3-4 minutes, or until cooked through. Remove with a slotted spoon and keep warm.

In the oil remaining in the pan, fry the onion, garlic and chilli for 3 minutes. Add the ginger, coriander, sugar, soy sauce, tomato paste and salt to taste with 3 tablespoons of water and simmer for 3 minutes.

Return the crab claws to the pan, add the lime juice, stir to coat thoroughly and simmer for 1-2 minutes, stirring until well heated through.'

'MALAYSIAN MILD CURRY PASTE' is sold in many supermarkets. If unavailable, substitute another strong curry paste or a mild Malaysian curry powder.

MUSSELS WITH CURRIED COCONUT NOODLES

1 k/2¼ lb cleaned mussels in their shells
300 ml/½ pt coconut cream
192 g/7 oz jar Sharwood's 'Malaysian mild curry paste'
250 g/8½ oz Chinese noodles
curls of fresh coconut, peeled with a swivel vegetable peeler, to garnish
chopped coriander, to garnish (optional)

Soak the mussels in cold water for at least 1 hour to remove any traces of dirt or sand, changing the water at least 3 times. Drain the mussels and give any which remain open a sharp tap. Those which do not close again are dead and must be thrown away.

Put the coconut cream and the curry paste in a large saucepan which has a tight-fitting lid and place over a moderate heat, stirring gently. Add the mussels, cover the pan and cook for about 5 minutes, shaking the pan occasionally, until all the shells have opened. (Those few which do not should also be discarded.) Do not overcook or the mussels will become tough and rubbery.

Meanwhile, cook the noodles in boiling water, according to the instructions on the packet, and then drain them thoroughly.

To serve: divide the noodles between 6 warmed bowls or dishes and pour over the mussels and sauce. Sprinkle with coconut curls and chopped coriander, if using, and serve immediately.

Top: Mussels with Curried Coconut Noodles; bottom: Spiced Crab Claws

For the CRISPY
SESAME PRAWNS *it
is important to keep
the tails attached to
the prawns when
peeling them. They
then look much more
attractive when
cooked and are easier
to dip in the sauce
and eat.*

CRISPY SESAME PRAWNS

225 g/8 oz raw prawns, peeled
vegetable oil, for deep-frying
sweet chilli sauce or other dipping sauce, to serve
FOR THE BATTER
85 g/3 oz flour
3 tbsp cornflour
1 tsp baking powder
¼ tsp chilli powder
½ tsp salt
1 tbsp vegetable oil
2 tbsp sesame seeds

At least 1 hour ahead, make the batter by thoroughly mixing the flour, cornflour, baking powder and chilli powder with 175 ml/6 fl oz water in a bowl. Leave this batter to rest for at least 1 hour.

Just before using, beat the salt and the oil into the batter until well incorporated and then stir in the sesame seeds.

Dip the prawns in the batter and deep-fry them a few at a time in hot oil in a wok. Drain on paper towels and keep warm while the rest are being cooked.

Serve as soon as all the prawns are cooked, accompanied by a dipping sauce, such as sweet chilli sauce or a mixture of equal parts light soy sauce and malt or white wine vinegar.

INDONESIAN SQUID

1 tbsp vegetable oil
1 small onion, chopped
2 garlic cloves, crushed
2.5 cm/1 in cube of peeled fresh root ginger, finely chopped
½ tsp chilli powder
grated zest and juice of 1 unwaxed lime
1 tbsp soft brown sugar
400 ml/14 fl oz thick coconut milk
12 small prepared squid, sacs sliced into thin rings
salt
chopped coriander, to garnish

Heat the oil in a saucepan or wok over a moderate heat and fry the onion, garlic and ginger for 2-3 minutes.

Add the chilli powder, lime zest and juice, the sugar and some salt to taste. Stir to mix well, then add the coconut milk. Simmer for 10 minutes.

Add the squid tentacles and slices and simmer for 10 minutes. Do not overcook or it will become tough and rubbery.

Serve sprinkled with chopped coriander.

Ready-prepared
SQUID *are available fresh from better fishmongers and frozen from Oriental supermarkets.*

Top: Sesame-crumbed Salmon with Ginger Cream (page 28); bottom: Crispy Sesame Prawns

CRISPY DUCK WITH PANCAKES

SERVES 4–6

1 dressed duck, weighing 1.8–2 k/4–4½ lb, giblets
removed
24 small ready-made Chinese pancakes
salt
bottled hoi-sin sauce, to serve
4 spring onions, cut into small sticks, to serve
¼ cucumber, cut into small sticks, to serve

At least 6 hours ahead, pour a large kettle of boiling water over the duck. This will tighten the skin. Then dry the bird thoroughly inside and out, place it on a rack and leave in an airy place for at least 6 hours, but preferably up to 12.

Preheat the oven to 180C/350F/gas4.

Prick the skin of the duck all over with a skewer to allow the fat to escape during cooking, then rub the skin all over with salt.

Place the bird on a rack over a roasting tin and roast for 2 hours. The flesh will become very tender and the skin very crisp.

To serve: pull the meat off the carcass and shred this and the skin by pulling it apart with two forks. Arrange the meat and skin on a warmed serving plate and keep warm.

Warm the pancakes through for a couple of minutes in a steamer and then serve these on a warmed serving plate. Serve the sauce, the spring onions and cucumber in separate bowls.

Each pancake is spread with a little sauce. A few pieces of spring onion and cucumber are then arranged on top of this, followed by some of the duck flesh and some of the crispy skin. The pancake is then rolled up and eaten with the fingers. Be sure to provide plenty of napkins and finger-bowls.

CHINESE PANCAKES *for this well-loved dish are available ready-made in packets from Chinese supermarkets.*

The recipe for
BALINESE-STYLE
DUCK *was given to
me by a dance teacher
in whose house I
stayed on Bali. I
have had to adapt it
slightly, as not all
the spices used are
available in the
West.*

BALINESE-STYLE DUCK

SERVES 6 AS A MAIN COURSE

1 dressed duck, weighing 1.8–2 k/4–4½ lb, with giblets
1½ tsp salt
½ tsp chilli powder
½ tsp ground cumin
½ tsp ground coriander
6 hard-boiled eggs, quartered, to serve
deep-fried onion rings, to garnish (optional)
FOR THE SAUCE
1 tbsp vegetable oil
1 small onion, chopped
1 garlic clove, crushed
*2.5 cm/1 in cube of peeled fresh root ginger, crushed
through a garlic press or very finely chopped*
1 chilli pepper, deseeded and chopped
grated zest and juice of 1 unwaxed lemon
2 tsp brown sugar
300 ml/½ pt coconut cream
2 tsp soy sauce

At least 6 hours ahead, remove the giblets from the duck and set them aside. Pour a large kettle of boiling water over the duck. This will tighten the skin. Then dry the bird thoroughly inside and out, place it on a rack and leave in an airy place for at least 6 hours, but preferably up to 12.

Put the giblets in a small pan, add just enough water to cover and bring to the boil, skimming off any scum which rises to the surface. Cover and simmer for 1 hour. Discard the giblets and boil the stock hard until reduced to about 2 tablespoons of concentrated essence. Set aside.

Preheat the oven to 180C/350F/gas4.

Prick the skin of the duck all over with a skewer to let the fat run during cooking. Mix 1 teaspoon of the salt with the chilli powder, cumin and coriander and rub this all over the skin. Place the bird on a rack over a roasting tin and roast in the oven for 2 hours.

The skin will become crisp and golden.

Towards the end of this time, make the sauce: heat the oil in a saucepan over a moderate heat and cook the onion until translucent. Add the reduced stock together with the garlic, ginger, chilli, lemon zest and juice, sugar, coconut cream, soy sauce and remaining salt. Bring to the boil, cover the pan and simmer for 30 minutes.

When the duck is cooked, remove from the oven and allow it to rest for 10 minutes. Remove all the skin, cut it into bite-sized pieces and set aside.

Remove the meat and cut into bite-sized pieces. Toss in the sauce to coat thoroughly.

Transfer to a warmed serving dish, surround with the egg quarters, sprinkle over the crispy skin pieces and garnish with the fried onion rings, if using. Serve with plainly cooked white rice.

JAPANESE DEEP-FRIED CHICKEN

450 g/1 lb chicken breast fillet, cut into 3 cm/1¼ in cubes
cornflour, for dusting
vegetable oil, for deep-frying
*1 green sweet pepper, deseeded and cut into strips,
to garnish*
FOR THE MARINADE
2 tbsp soy sauce
1 tbsp sake, sherry or white wine
1 garlic clove, crushed
*juice from a 3 cm/1¼ in cube of peeled fresh root ginger,
crushed through a garlic press*

Make the marinade: mix the ingredients in a bowl. Add the chicken pieces, mix well and leave to marinate for 1 hour, stirring occasionally.

Drain the chicken thoroughly, discarding the marinade. Toss the pieces of chicken in cornflour and shake off any excess. Deep-fry them in batches in hot oil in a wok for 3-4 minutes each, until golden brown and crispy. Drain on paper towels and keep each batch warm while cooking the rest.

When all the chicken is cooked, arrange on a warmed serving plate, surround with the pepper strips and serve immediately.

LEMON CHICKEN

white of 1 egg, lightly beaten
3 tsp cornflour
285 g/10 oz chicken breast fillet, cut across into 1 cm/½ in strips
6 tbsp chicken stock
juice of 1 lemon
2 tsp sugar
2 tsp light soy sauce
2 tsp sherry
1 garlic clove, crushed
pinch of chilli powder
½ small green sweet pepper, deseeded and cut into even bite-sized pieces
vegetable oil, for deep-frying

Mix the egg white with 2 teaspoons of the cornflour thoroughly in a bowl. Then mix in the chicken strips, making sure they are all well coated. Cover with film and chill for 30 minutes.

Deep-fry the chicken in hot oil in a wok for 1 minute, then drain on paper towels. Keep warm.

In a bowl, mix together the stock, lemon juice, sugar, soy sauce, sherry, garlic and chilli powder.

Leave 1 tablespoon of oil in the wok and stir-fry the pepper for 2 minutes over a moderate heat. Stir in the stock mixture and simmer for 1 minute.

Mix the remaining cornflour with 1 tablespoon of water, add this to the pan and simmer for 1 more minute, stirring. Return the chicken to the pan and stir-fry for about 30 seconds. Serve immediately.

STICKY CHICKEN

8 chicken wings
3 garlic cloves, crushed
4 cm/1½ in cube of peeled fresh root ginger, crushed through a garlic press or very finely chopped
juice of 1 lemon
2 tbsp soy sauce
2 tbsp runny honey
½ tsp chilli powder

Divide each chicken wing into pieces by cutting through the joints. Discard any pointed wing tip pieces or use for stock. There should be 16 pieces left.

Combine all the remaining ingredients in a shallow ovenproof dish large enough to accommodate the chicken pieces snugly in 1 layer. Add the chicken and mix to coat thoroughly.

Cover with film and marinate for at least 2 hours in a cool place or up to 24 in the refrigerator.

Preheat the oven to 220C/425F/gas7.

Remove the film, turn the chicken pieces once more in the marinade and put the dish in the oven. Cook for 20 minutes, turning and basting halfway through. The chicken will be cooked through and coated with a delicious sticky glaze.

These pieces of chicken wing are best eaten with the fingers, so supply plenty of napkins and finger-bowls.

SAKE *is the rice wine of Japan and is much used in their cooking. Sherry makes a good substitute.*

Chicken drumsticks or thighs also work well in the STICKY CHICKEN *recipe.*

CHICKEN WITH STRAW MUSHROOM CURRY

4 skinned chicken breast fillets
2 tbsp vegetable oil
salt and freshly ground black pepper
FOR THE SAUCE
2 tbsp vegetable oil
1 onion, chopped
1 garlic clove, crushed
1 stalk of lemon grass, finely chopped
1 chilli pepper, deseeded and chopped
¼ tsp ground cinnamon
½ tsp ground cardamom
1 heaped tsp curry powder
300 ml/½ pt coconut cream
425 g/15 oz canned straw mushrooms, drained
juice of ½ lemon

If you can't find lemon grass for the CHICKEN WITH STRAW MUSHROOM CURRY, *substitute the grated rind of half a lemon or lime. Small egg-shaped* STRAW MUSHROOMS *are rarely seen fresh in the West, but are readily available canned from Oriental shops.*

First make the sauce: heat the oil in saucepan over a moderate heat and cook the onion with the garlic and lemon grass, stirring occasionally, for 4–5 minutes, or until the onion has softened.

Add the chilli, dry spices and curry powder. Stir-fry for 1 minute. Add the coconut cream and simmer for another 5 minutes.

Purée the sauce in a blender or food processor and return it to the pan. Add the mushrooms and simmer for 2–3 minutes, or until they are warmed through. Stir in the lemon juice and a pinch of salt.

Meanwhile, season the chicken lightly. Heat the oil in a frying pan over a moderate heat and fry the fillets gently for 3–4 minutes on each side, or until golden brown and cooked through.

Arrange the cooked chicken on a warmed serving platter and spoon over the sauce. If serving as part of a meal to be eaten with chopsticks, slice the chicken across into into bite-sized pieces before serving it.

CHICKEN WITH CASHEW NUTS

170 g/6 oz lean skinless chicken, cut into bite-sized pieces
30 g/1 oz carrot, sliced
2 tbsp vegetable oil
55 g/2 oz unsalted cashew nuts
30 g/1 oz canned bamboo shoots, sliced
1 tbsp frozen peas
FOR THE MARINADE
2 tbsp cornflour
1 tsp vegetable oil
FOR THE SAUCE
1 tsp soy sauce
1 tsp dry sherry
½ tsp cornflour
pinch of salt

First make the marinade: in a small bowl, mix together the cornflour and oil with 2 tablespoons of water. Add the chicken, mix well and leave to marinate for 10 minutes.

Blanch the carrot slices in boiling salted water for 2 minutes. Drain.

Heat a wok until it is very hot, then add the oil and stir-fry the chicken for 3–4 minutes, until cooked through.

Add the carrot, nuts, bamboo shoots and peas and stir-fry for another minute.

Mix the sauce ingredients together with 4 tablespoons of water. Add this to the pan and cook for another minute or so, until the sauce has thickened. Serve immediately.

Top: Chicken with Straw Mushroom Curry served with plainly cooked noodles; bottom: Chicken with Cashew Nuts

Nuts like almonds or walnuts also work well in place of the cashews in the recipe for CHICKEN WITH CASHEW NUTS.

STUFFED BEAN CURD

MAKES 8

block of firm tofu, weighing about 675 g/1½ lb
3 tbsp vegetable oil
250 ml/8 fl oz chicken stock
½ tsp salt
1 generous tbsp Chinese oyster sauce
1 tsp cornflour, mixed with a little water, plus more
for dusting
2 thinly sliced spring onions, to garnish
FOR THE STUFFING
115 g/4 oz minced chicken
1 tbsp finely chopped onion
2 tbsp light soy sauce
1½ tsp cornflour

First make the stuffing by mixing together the ingredients in a bowl.

Cut the tofu into 4 equal portions which will measure about 10 cm/4 in square by 3 cm/1¼ in thick. Now cut these diagonally across to make triangular wedges. Using a sharp knife, cut a slit into the long side of each wedge and scoop out a little of the tofu to make a pocket to take the stuffing. Be careful not to cut too deeply, and work very carefully as the tofu is very fragile.

Dust the insides of each pocket with a little cornflour and carefully fill with the stuffing.

Heat the oil in a pan wide enough to take the pieces of curd in one layer (a sauté pan or deep-frying pan is ideal) over a very low heat. Place them in the pan with the stuffed side down and cook for about 5 minutes, until the stuffing is golden brown.

Pour in the stock, cover the pan and simmer for 3 minutes. Remove the tofu and keep warm.

Add the salt, oyster sauce, and cornflour mixture to the pan and simmer until thickened.

Arrange the tofu on a warmed serving plate, pour over the sauce and garnish with spring onion.

SPICED BEEF

SERVES 4–6

2 tbsp vegetable oil
900 g/2 lb piece of rolled topside or brisket of beef
2 tbsp soy sauce
4 tbsp sherry
2 garlic cloves, crushed
3 heads of star anise
1 tbsp sugar
3 carrots, thinly sliced
30 g/1 oz butter
1 tsp Oriental sesame oil
2 tsp lemon juice
1 tsp black mustard seeds
salt and freshly ground black pepper

Heat the vegetable oil in a saucepan which has a tight-fitting lid and is just large enough to fit the piece of meat snugly. Brown the meat on all sides.

Add the soy sauce, sherry, garlic and star anise. Cover the pan tightly and cook over a very low heat, undisturbed, for 1 hour.

Add the sugar and a good grinding of black pepper, replace the lid and continue to cook for 1 more hour.

Lift the meat out of the pan and allow it to rest for 10 minutes. Meanwhile, boil the liquid in the pan rapidly to reduce it to a sticky sauce.

At the same time, steam the carrots until just tender. Melt the butter with the sesame oil in a saucepan over a moderate heat and add the lemon juice, mustard seeds and a pinch of salt. Toss the steamed carrots in this to coat thoroughly.

Cut the meat into slices and arrange them on a warmed serving platter. Drizzle over the sauce and surround the meat with the carrots. Serve accompanied by plainly cooked white rice.

The SPICED BEEF *is also delicious served cold and sliced as part of a picnic or in sandwiches.*

CRUMBED GINGER STEAKS

2 sirloin steaks, each weighing about 170 g/6 oz
1 tbsp soy sauce
1 tbsp sherry or white wine
1 garlic clove, crushed
2.5 cm/1 in cube of peeled fresh root ginger, crushed
through a garlic press
1 egg, beaten
55 g/2 oz fine fresh white breadcrumbs
3 tbsp vegetable oil
flour, for coating
chopped spring onions, to garnish

Cut each steak in half to make 4 equal pieces in all. Place these between 2 sheets of film, and flatten them with a rolling pin until they are as thin as possible. They should at least double in size.

Mix together the soy sauce, sherry or wine, garlic and ginger in a wide bowl and then put the flattened steaks into it. Mix well so that all surfaces of the meat are coated. Cover with film and leave in the refrigerator for at least 6 hours or up to 24.

Drain the marinated steaks well and pat them dry with paper towels.

Put some flour, the beaten egg and the breadcrumbs in 3 separate shallow dishes. Dip the pieces of steak first in flour, then shake off any excess. Then dip them in the beaten egg and finally the breadcrumbs.

Heat the oil in a frying pan (not a wok) over a moderate to high heat and fry the pieces of steak, in batches if necessary, for 1–2 minutes on each side, or until the crumbs are crisp and golden.

Serve Western-style, with plain rice or potatoes and vegetables, or slice the steaks into strips and serve as part of an Oriental-style meal. Either way, garnish with the chopped spring onions.

STIR-FRIED BEEF WITH CELERY

3 tbsp soy sauce
2 garlic cloves, crushed
2 tsp cornflour
1 tsp sugar
450 g/1 lb sirloin or rump steak, cut into thin bite-sized
strips
3 tbsp vegetable oil
225 g/8 oz celery, cut across at an angle into thin slices
4 cm/1½ in cube of peeled fresh root ginger, thinly sliced

Combine the soy sauce, garlic, cornflour and sugar in a small bowl and then add the beef strips and mix well until each piece is coated. Leave to marinate for 20-30 minutes.

Heat the oil in a wok or frying pan over a moderate heat and add the meat mixture. Stir-fry for 3-4 minutes.

Add the slices of celery and ginger and continue to stir-fry the mixture for 4 minutes more. Serve immediately.

Based on a traditional Japanese dish, CRUMBED GINGER STEAKS is a simple and unusual way to cook steak. It also allows a little expensive meat to go a long way, so it is worth buying the best quality beef.

SWEET-AND-SOUR SPARE RIBS

1.35 k/3 lb pork spare ribs
2 tbsp soy sauce
3 tbsp tomato ketchup
6 tbsp orange juice
2 tbsp white or red wine vinegar
2 tbsp soft brown sugar
1 tsp salt
2 garlic cloves, crushed
2.5 cm/1 in cube of peeled fresh root ginger, very finely chopped
¼ tsp chilli powder
freshly ground black pepper

Separate the ribs by cutting down between the bones and put the pieces in a wide ovenproof dish or baking tray.

Combine the remaining ingredients, season well with pepper and pour over the ribs. Mix well so that each rib is coated. Cover and leave to marinate for at least 6 hours, or up to 24 in the refrigerator.

Preheat the oven to 180C/350F/gas4.

Bake the ribs, uncovered, for 1½ hours, basting them every 15–20 minutes. Increase the oven setting to 220C/425F/gas7 and cook the ribs for another 30 minutes, turning them over after 15 minutes. The liquid will have almost entirely evaporated, leaving the ribs a deep mahogany brown and covered in a delicious sticky glaze.

These ribs are best eaten with the fingers, so supply lots of napkins and finger-bowls.

Left to right: Stir-fried Beef with Celery (page 41), Stuffed Bean Curd (page 40) and Sweet-and-Sour Spare Ribs

PORK WITH NOODLES, MUSHROOMS AND SPINACH

350 g/12 oz Chinese noodles
3 tbsp vegetable oil
½ small onion, finely chopped
2.5 cm/1 in cube of peeled fresh root ginger, finely chopped
2 garlic cloves, finely chopped
2 red or green chilli peppers, deseeded and finely chopped,
plus extra for garnish (optional)
450 g/1 lb lean pork, cut into thin bite-sized strips
170 g/6 oz firm mushrooms, thinly sliced
4 tbsp white wine or pale stock
350 g/12 oz spinach, torn into smallish shreds
salt and freshly ground black pepper

There is a wide variety of very different types of CHINESE NOODLES, *which require varying degrees of cooking. Always check the packet for cooking times.*

First cook the noodles according to the instructions on the packet. Drain them well and then toss them in 1 tablespoon of the oil to prevent them from sticking together.

Heat the remaining oil in a wok or large saucepan over a high heat and stir-fry the onion for 1 minute. Add the ginger, garlic and chilli peppers and continue to stir-fry for 1 more minute.

Add the pork strips and mushrooms and continue to stir-fry for 3-4 minutes, or until the meat is cooked and the mushrooms are beginning to soften.

Season with salt and pepper, pour in the wine or stock, add the spinach and sir-fry just until the spinach begins to wilt. Do not over-cook: each piece of spinach should still retain some shape and stay separate rather than sticking together in a mush.

Add the cooked noodles to the stir-fried mixture and continue to cook for another 1-2 minutes, until the ingredients are well mixed together and the noodles are really hot.

Serve immediately in 4 warmed bowls and garnish with extra chopped chilli peppers, if using.

Note: if good fresh spinach is unobtainable, use spring greens or Cos lettuce.

BALINESE PORK

2 tbsp vegetable oil
450 g/1 lb pork fillet, cut into 2 cm/¾ in cubes
1 onion, finely chopped
3 garlic cloves, finely chopped
1 chilli pepper or more to taste, deseeded and finely chopped
1 tsp ground coriander
1 tsp turmeric
1 tsp cornflour
300 ml/½ pt coconut cream
1 tsp salt

Heat half the oil in a wok or saucepan which has a tight-fitting lid over a moderate heat and stir-fry the pork for 3-4 minutes or so, until the meat is coloured all over. Using a slotted spoon, remove the pork from the pan and set aside.

Add the remaining oil to the pan and stir-fry the onion for 3-4 minutes or until softened. Add the garlic, chilli, coriander and turmeric and continue to stir-fry for another 2-3 minutes. Return the pork to the pan .

Dissolve the cornflour in 1 tablespoon of water and stir this into the coconut cream. Add this to the pan and bring it to the boil. Add the salt and simmer, covered, over the lowest possible heat for about an hour, or until the meat is tender.

Transfer to a warmed dish to serve.

Pork with Noodles, Mushrooms and Spinach

VEGETABLES, SALADS, RICE AND NOODLES

Vegetables in every form feature heavily in all Oriental cuisines and are considered important ingredients in their own right, rather than as mere fillers, accompaniments or garnishes as is so often the case in much of the cooking of the West. Rice and noodles are treated with even greater respect and form the central part of most Oriental meals, from breakfast to lavish banquets. These staples are usually served plainly cooked as a perfect bland background for the other more highly flavoured cooked dishes, but they are occasionally given more elaborate treatment with other ingredients in order to play a more prominent starring role in a meal.

Left: Japanese-style Chicken and Asparagus Salad (page 48); right: Thai Chicken, Prawn and Fruit Salad (page 48)

THAI CHICKEN, PRAWN AND FRUIT SALAD

*½ mango or papaya, peeled, stoned or deseeded and cut into
bite-sized pieces
1 orange, peeled and segmented
1 small grapefruit, preferably pink, peeled and segmented
1 pear, peeled, cored and cut into bite-sized pieces
16 seedless grapes, halved
8 lychees, peeled and stoned
2 tomatoes, cut into small pieces
115 g/4 oz canned Chinese water chestnuts, drained
and halved
170 g/6 oz cooked chicken, cut into bite-sized pieces
115 g/4 oz peeled cooked prawns
55 g/2 oz mixed salad leaves
4-6 shallots, thinly sliced
2 garlic cloves, thinly sliced
115 g/4 oz salted peanuts, roughly chopped, to garnish
coriander sprigs, to garnish (optional)*
FOR THE DRESSING
*3 tbsp sugar
juice of ½ lime
1 tbsp fish sauce
1 red chilli pepper, deseeded and chopped
1 garlic clove, crushed*

The classic THAI
CHICKEN, PRAWN
AND FRUIT SALAD
*makes a spectacular
first course or light
meal. Any fruit in
season may be used
and those given here
are merely
suggestions.*

In a bowl, mix together lightly the fruit, tomatoes, water chestnuts, chicken and prawns.

Make the dressing: dissolve the sugar in 5 tablespoons of hot water and allow it to cool. Then mix in the lime juice, fish sauce, chilli and garlic.

Deep-fry the shallot and garlic slices in hot oil in a wok until crisp. Drain on paper towels.

Just before serving, pour the dressing over the salad and mix gently.

Cover a serving plate with the leaves and arrange the salad over this. Scatter over the fried shallots and garlic and the peanuts and coriander sprigs, if using, to garnish. Serve immediately.

JAPANESE-STYLE CHICKEN AND ASPARAGUS SALAD

*1 tbsp sake, sherry or white wine
½ tsp salt
about 225 g/8 oz skinless chicken breast fillets, cut across
into thin slices
450 g/1 lb asparagus, cut across at an angle into
3.5 cm/1½ in lengths
salad leaves, to serve (optional)
1 tsp very thin julienne strips of thinly pared zest from an
unwaxed lemon, to garnish*
FOR THE DRESSING
*1 tsp dry English mustard powder
2 tbsp sake, sherry or white wine
2 tbsp soy sauce*

In a small bowl, mix the sake, sherry or wine with the salt. Toss the chicken pieces in this and leave to marinate for 30 minutes.

Bring 5 tablespoons of water to the boil in the bottom of a wok or very small heavy-based saucepan and cook the chicken pieces, stirring constantly, for 1-2 minutes or until just cooked. Using a slotted spoon, transfer the chicken to a bowl and allow to cool. Reserve the stock left in the pan for making the dressing and for adding to soups and sauces.

Cook the asparagus in boiling salted water for 3-4 minutes, or until just cooked but still firm. Immediately drain and refresh under cold running water, then drain again. Add to the chicken.

Make the dressing: mix together the ingredients with 1 tablespoon of the reserved stock.

Just before serving, pour the dressing over the salad and toss well to combine thoroughly. Transfer to a serving plate or dish and serve as part of an Oriental-style meal. Alternatively, make 4 individual servings piled on beds of salad leaves, if using, and serve as a Western-style first course. Either way, garnish with the lemon zest.

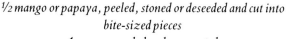

STIR-FRIED VEGETABLES

2 tbsp vegetable oil
1 garlic clove, thinly sliced
2.5 cm/1 in cube of peeled fresh root ginger, finely chopped
1 chilli pepper, deseeded and chopped (optional)
1 small onion, chopped
1 small carrot, cut across at an angle into slices
½ red, green or yellow sweet pepper, deseeded and cut into uniform bite-sized pieces
115 g/4 oz sugar peas or mange-tout peas
55 g/2 oz canned straw mushrooms, drained
1 tsp cornflour
1 tbsp soy sauce
chopped spring onion, chives or fresh coriander, to garnish (optional)

Heat a wok or large frying pan over a moderate heat and add the oil. When it is really hot, add the garlic, ginger and chilli, if using, and stir-fry the mixture for 1 minute.

Add the onion, carrot, and sweet pepper and stir-fry for another 2–3 minutes. Add the sugar peas or mange-tout peas and the straw mushrooms and stir-fry the vegetables for 2 more minutes.

Mix the cornflour with the soy sauce and then stir this into 125 ml/4 fl oz of water. Pour this liquid over the hot vegetables and allow it to bubble up and thicken while continuing to stir-fry for a few seconds.

Immediately transfer to a warmed serving dish and garnish with spring onions or herbs, if using.

STIR-FRIED BEANS WITH GARLIC

2 tbsp vegetable oil
½ tsp salt
4 garlic cloves, coarsely chopped
2.5 cm/1 in cube of peeled fresh root ginger, finely chopped
450 g/1 lb green beans, cut into 7.5 cm/3 in lengths
125 ml/4 fl oz chicken stock

Heat a wok over a moderate heat until hot, add the oil with the salt, garlic and ginger and stir-fry for 30 seconds.

Add the green beans and stock and continue to cook for 4 minutes, or until the beans are just tender and most of the liquid has evaporated.

Serve at once.

Stir-frying is the ideal healthy way to cook most vegetables. Use whatever is fresh and in season and try to make the best combination of colours, textures and flavours.

The SWEET
POTATO, *a tuber
related to the potato,
tastes a little like a
cross between a
turnip and a chestnut
and is now readily
available in many
food markets and
supermarkets.*

MUSHROOM CURRY WITH QUAILS' EGGS

*2 tbsp vegetable oil
1 onion, chopped
1 garlic clove, crushed
2.5 cm/1 in cube of peeled fresh root ginger, finely chopped
1 stalk of lemon grass, finely chopped
2 chilli peppers or more to taste, finely chopped
grated zest and juice of 1 unwaxed lime
1 tbsp finely chopped fresh coriander stems
1 tsp salt
225 g/8 oz small button mushrooms
425 g/15 oz canned straw mushrooms, drained
300 ml/½ pt coconut cream
24 hard-boiled quails' eggs, shelled
chopped coriander, to garnish (optional)
chopped chilli peppers, to garnish (optional)*

Heat the oil in a heavy-based saucepan over a moderate heat and cook the onion until it is softened.

Add the garlic, ginger, lemon grass, chilli peppers, lime zest, coriander stems and salt. Cook for 1-2 minutes, stirring constantly.

Add the button mushrooms and cook for 3-4 minutes, or until they are just beginning to soften.

Add the straw mushrooms and the coconut cream and simmer, stirring occasionally, for about 30 minutes.

Add the quails' eggs and lime juice and cook for 1-2 minutes longer, or until the eggs are heated through.

Pour into a warmed serving dish and garnish with chopped coriander and chilli peppers, if using.

CURRIED SWEET POTATO

*1 tbsp vegetable oil
1 onion, chopped
1 garlic clove, crushed
grated zest of ½ unwaxed lemon
2.5 cm/1 in piece of peeled fresh root ginger, finely chopped
or crushed through a garlic press
1 tbsp curry powder
1 tsp turmeric
300 ml/½ pt coconut cream
675 g/1½ lb sweet potato, peeled and cut into
2.5 cm/1 in cubes
½ tsp salt
5 tbsp natural yogurt
85 g/3 oz dry roasted peanuts, roughly chopped, to garnish
finely chopped coriander or flat-leaf parsley, to garnish*

Heat the oil in a heavy-based saucepan over a moderate heat and cook the onion until translucent. Add the garlic, lemon zest, ginger and spices and stir-fry for 2-3 minutes. Stir in the coconut cream and continue to cook for 15 minutes over a gentle heat, stirring occasionally.

Meanwhile, sprinkle the sweet potato with the salt and steam it for about 15 minutes until just tender. Do not over-cook.

Stir the yogurt into the sauce. Heat through, but do not allow to boil. Mix the sweet potato into the curry sauce.

Transfer to a warmed serving dish or platter and garnish with the chopped peanuts and herbs.

Top: Curried Sweet Potato; bottom: Mushroom Curry with Quails' Eggs served on a bed of noodles

The classic Japanese batter used in TEMPURA VEGETABLES *produces the lightest possible coating. Use whatever selection of vegetables you fancy, or try slivers of meat or fish or raw prawns, as the Japanese also do.*

FRIED NOODLES WITH VEGETABLES

8 dried Chinese mushrooms
350 g/12 oz Oriental noodles
3 tbsp vegetable oil
1 garlic clove, thinly sliced
2.5 cm/1 in cube of peeled fresh root ginger, finely chopped
1 onion, chopped
1 small carrot, cut across at an angle into slices
½ green sweet pepper, deseeded and cut into bite-sized pieces
55 g/2 oz cabbage, sliced
1 tbsp soy sauce
1 tbsp sesame oil
2 tbsp raw shelled peanuts, chopped

Cover the dried mushrooms with hot water and leave them to soak for 30 minutes. Strain and remove the hard stalk (this may be either discarded or used to add flavour to stock). Slice the mushroom caps and reserve.

Cook the noodles according to the instructions on the packet and then drain well.

Heat the oil in a wok or large frying pan over a moderate heat and stir-fry the garlic and ginger for 1 minute. Add the onion and stir-fry for 2-3 minutes more. Then add the carrot, pepper, cabbage and sliced mushrooms caps and stir-fry for 2-3 minutes.

Add the cooked and drained noodles and continue to cook, tossing all the ingredients together for 2-3 minutes, or until all the noodles are thoroughly heated through.

Stir in the soy sauce and sesame oil and sprinkle over the chopped nuts to serve.

Tempura Vegetables

TEMPURA VEGETABLES

1 egg plus 1 extra yolk, beaten
115 g/4 oz flour
about 225 g/8 oz mixed vegetables, such as courgettes, asparagus tips, broccoli and cauliflower florets, baby spinach leaves, carrots and deseeded sweet peppers, cut into bite-sized pieces
vegetable oil, for deep-frying

In a bowl, make a smooth batter with the egg, flour and 175 ml/6 fl oz of water.

Dip the pieces of vegetable into the batter and deep-fry them in hot oil in a wok a few at a time. Drain on paper towels and serve immediately as they are cooked, just as they are or with a dipping sauce.

NOTE: an excellent dipping sauce for this dish may be made from equal quantities of soy sauce, fish sauce and sherry, together with a little added grated fresh root ginger.

Gado Gado, a salad of cooked and raw vegetables with a spicy peanut dressing, is perhaps the best-known of all Indonesian dishes. Nasi Goreng, another typically Indonesian dish, consists of fried rice with chicken and prawns – often topped with a fried egg or omelette – and is virtually a meal in itself. However, served together the two dishes make a wonderful well-balanced meal.

NASI GORENG

350 g/12 oz rice
2 tbsp vegetable oil
115 g/4 oz skinless chicken breast, cut into small cubes
1 onion, chopped
2 garlic cloves, finely chopped
2.5 cm/1 in cube of peeled fresh root ginger, finely chopped
1 chilli pepper, deseeded and finely chopped
½ tsp ground coriander
2 tbsp soy sauce
1 tbsp sugar
115 g/4 oz peeled cooked prawns
1 egg, beaten, to garnish (optional)
cucumber slices, to garnish
prawn crackers, to garnish (optional)

About an hour or two ahead, cook the rice in boiling salted water until tender. Drain, if necessary, and then leave it to cool. This dish may be made successfully with leftover cooked rice, but it is much better if the rice is freshly cooked.

Heat the oil in a wok or large frying pan over a moderate heat and stir-fry the chicken and onion, together with the garlic, ginger, chilli and coriander, for 3-4 minutes, or until the chicken is cooked and the onion slightly softened.

Add the soy sauce, sugar and prawns and stir-fry for 1 minute. Tip in the rice and stir-fry for 2-3 minutes more.

If using the egg garnish, heat a very little oil in a small frying pan over a moderate heat and cook the beaten egg in it until just set. Then cut this omelette into strips.

Serve immediately, topped with the omelette strips, if using, and garnished with cucumber slices and prawn crackers if using.

GADO GADO

350 g/12 oz cabbage, shredded
140 g/5 oz green beans
350 g/12 oz beansprouts
4 small cooked new potatoes, sliced or quartered
¼ cucumber, sliced
2 hard-boiled eggs, shelled and sliced or cut in small wedges
prawn crackers, to garnish (optional)
FOR THE SAUCE
1 tbsp vegetable oil
1 small onion, chopped
1 garlic clove, crushed
1 tsp chilli powder
grated zest and 2 tsp of juice from ½ small unwaxed lemon
2 tsp brown sugar
1 tsp soy sauce
½ tsp salt
125 ml/4 fl oz coconut cream
3 tbsp smooth peanut butter

First make the sauce: heat the oil in a saucepan over a moderate heat and cook the onion with the garlic until translucent. Add the rest of the sauce ingredients with 6 tablespoons of water and simmer gently for 15 minutes, stirring frequently and making sure the peanut butter dissolves. Allow to cool.

In a large pan of boiling salted water, blanch the cabbage and beans for 3 minutes and then blanch the beansprouts for 30 seconds only. Drain and refresh each batch under cold running water as soon as it is cooked. Drain again thoroughly and pat dry.

When the sauce is cool, arrange all the salad ingredients attractively in layers on a serving dish or on 4 small plates, spoon over the sauce, and garnish with prawn crackers, if using.

Top: Nasi Goreng; bottom: Gado Gado

Translucent CELLOPHANE NOODLES are made from rice flour rather than wheat and have a very delicate flavour. Bottled CHINESE BLACK BEAN SAUCE, made from fermented beans, is a widely used condiment in Chinese kitchens and is available from Oriental shops and better supermarkets.

CELLOPHANE NOODLES WITH BLACK BEAN SAUCE

170 g/6 oz cellophane noodles
1 tbsp vegetable oil
1 large onion, thinly sliced
2 garlic cloves, crushed
300 ml/½ pt chicken stock
1 heaped tbsp Chinese black bean sauce
4 tsp light soy sauce
½ tsp chilli powder
1 scant tsp Oriental sesame oil

Soak the noodles in hot water for 10 minutes and then drain them well.

Heat the oil in a wok or large frying pan and stir-fry the onion for 2 minutes. Add the garlic, stock, sauces and chilli powder and simmer for 5 minutes.

Add the noodles and cook for 2 minutes, stirring constantly. (They will absorb most of the liquid.)

Sprinkle over the sesame oil, toss well and serve at once.

SPICY COCONUT RICE

SERVES 4–6

450 g/1 lb basmati rice
1 tbsp vegetable oil
1 large onion, chopped
2 garlic cloves, chopped
1 tsp dried coriander
1 tsp cumin
¼ tsp chilli powder
1½ tsp salt
450 ml/1 pt thin coconut milk
chopped fresh coriander or other herbs, to garnish

Wash the rice thoroughly and dry well.

In a large heavy-based saucepan which has a tight-fitting lid, heat the oil over a moderate heat and fry the onion until softened, Add the garlic, spices and salt and stir well. Add the rice and mix well until every grain is coated.

Add the coconut milk and bring to the boil. Turn the heat down to the lowest possible setting, put the lid tightly on the pan and cook undisturbed for 15 minutes.

Without removing the lid, leave the pan off the heat to allow the rice to finish cooking in the steam for a further 30 minutes.

Transfer to a serving dish and serve garnished with herbs.

Top: Spicy Coconut Rice; bottom: Cellophane Noodles with Black Bean Sauce

Of the many varieties of rice now widely available, basmati probably has the best flavour.

LAST COURSES

*I*n the cuisines of the countries of the Far East the boundary between sweet and savoury ingredients is much less marked than here in the West. For this reason, desserts, puddings and other sweet concoctions do not hold the same importance. Simple fresh fruit, in one form or another, usually makes the perfect refreshing finale to any Oriental meal. However, there follow a few of my favourite unusual and delicious traditional sweet dishes, usually incorporating fresh fruit, in order to satisfy the Western sweet tooth and round off any type of meal. If short of time, any good bought fruit-based ice-cream or sorbet will also work well. Serve it with canned or fresh exotic fruit, or sprinkled with green ginger wine or passion fruit pulp.

Left: Balinese-style Rice Pudding (page 61); right: Banana Pancake 'Noodles' (page 60)

KEBABS OF TROPICAL FRUIT

½ pineapple
1 banana
1 small wedge of water melon
1 mango
½ papaya
1 kiwi fruit
juice of 1 lemon or lime

Peel, core, stone and deseed the fruit as appropriate. Then cut them all into large bite-sized pieces.

Toss the fruit pieces in the lemon or lime juice to prevent discoloration.

Just before serving, thread the pieces of fruit alternately on wooden or metal skewers, contrasting colours attractively where possible.

BANANA PANCAKE 'NOODLES'

85 g/3 oz flour
pinch of salt
1 banana, peeled and mashed
2 eggs, beaten
150 ml/¼ pt milk
vegetable oil, for frying
sugar, to serve
juice of 1 lime, to serve
banana slices, to decorate (optional)

Mix the flour, salt, banana, eggs and milk into a batter. (This is most easily done in a blender or food processor.) Leave to rest for 1 hour.

Heat just enough oil in a medium-sized frying pan to coat the bottom with a thin film, then pour in one-quarter of the batter and cook over a fairly low heat until pale gold on both sides, turning once. Keep this pancake warm while making 3 others in the same way. They must be cooked over a low heat to allow the centres to cook through.

Roll each pancake up and quickly cut them across at 1 cm/½ in intervals. Then unroll the pieces to make long 'noodles'.

Make mounds of the 'noodles' on 4 warmed plates. Sprinkle with sugar and a squeeze of lime juice to serve decorated with banana slices, if using.

BALINESE-STYLE RICE PUDDING

575 ml/1 pt milk
300 ml/½ pt coconut cream
4 tbsp pudding rice
4 tbsp soft brown sugar
6 cardamom pods, split
30 g/1 oz butter, cut in small pieces, plus more for greasing
¼ tsp nutmeg
curls of fresh coconut, peeled with a swivel vegetable peeler, to garnish
salad of tropical fruits, such as mangoes, guavas, pineapples, bananas, limes and passion fruit, to serve

Preheat the oven to 150C/300F/gas2 and grease a shallow ovenproof dish with butter.

Put the milk, coconut cream, rice, sugar, cardamom pods and butter in the prepared dish and bake in the oven for 3 hours, stirring the contents of the dish every hour.

Remove from the oven, stir in the nutmeg and allow to cool. Chill until required.

Serve chilled, garnished with coconut curls and accompanied by tropical fruit salad.

ORANGES IN GREEN GINGER WINE

4 large oranges
about 150 ml/¼ pt green ginger wine
1 tbsp flaked almonds

Peel the oranges, removing all the bitter white pith, and slice across the segments as thinly as possible. Arrange the slices in the bottom of an attractive serving dish.

Pour over enough ginger wine almost to cover. Cover the bowl with film and chill for several hours, or overnight if possible.

Just before serving, sprinkle over the flaked almonds.

GREEN GINGER WINE *is a British brew widely available in off-licences and supermarkets. However, it does give a flavour quite like that of many Oriental preparations.*

Fresh lychees make the GUAVA JELLY WITH LYCHEES *even more memorable. In fact, any form of fresh or canned exotic fruit may be substituted.*

GUAVA JELLY WITH LYCHEES

400 g/14 oz canned guavas in syrup
2 sachets (2 tbsp) of powdered gelatine
400 g/14 oz canned lychees in syrup

Drain the syrup from the guavas, measure it and place in a bowl.

Following the instructions on the packet, dissolve half the gelatine in enough water to make the syrup up to 300 ml/½ pt. Mix this with the syrup and pour the mixture into a small wetted baking tin. Chill until set.

Meanwhile, purée the guavas in a blender or food processor and then strain the purée through a sieve.

Dissolve the rest of the gelatine in sufficient water to make the puréed guavas up to 300 ml/½ pt. Mix this with the purée, then pour this mixture over the jellied syrup mixture in the pan to make a second layer. Return to the refrigerator and chill the jelly until it is completely set, preferably overnight.

Dip the pan briefly in hot water and turn out the jelly. Using a hot wet knife, cut the jelly into cubes. Serve the cubes mixed with the lychees and their syrup.

Top: Oranges in Green Ginger Wine (page 61); bottom: Guava Jelly with Lychees

INDEX

ACKNOWLEDGEMENTS

The author would particularly like
to thank Michelle Garrett for
taking such wonderful
photographs, Mary Evans and Sue
Storey for designing the book so
beautifully and Ian Hands for his
invaluable help in preparing the
food for photography.
  He would also like to mention
the following mail-order supplier
of Oriental ingredients:

Exotic Speciality Food Limited,
20 Berkeley Street,
Hull HU3 1PR

The Publishers would like to thank
the following for the use of
accessories in the photography:

Sander Architectural Mirrors,
Sander House, Elmore Street,
London N1.

Neal Street East,
5 Neal Street,
London WC2